IMPERFECT GREATNESS

Bre'Yanna Mitriece

Published by Bre'Yanna M. Parker
©2014, Bre'Yanna M. Parker

ISBN-10-9780692200520
ISBN-13-0692200525

First Edition
First Printing, April 2014
10 9 8 7 6 5 4 3 2 1

Printed in the United States of America

Photography by ©J-ography
Dyamond Trimble
1018 Early Rise Ct
Raleigh, NC 27610
Contact Number: (919)539-6981
Jography22@gmail.com
Dyamondtrimble.wordpress.com

For Skye and Taighlor
"My Brown Queens, Everything I do is for you two"

For mommy and daddy
"Thanks for Life,
Encouragement and always loving me"

Table of Contents

Table of Contents

Imperfect Greatness

Brown Fleshed, big chest
A girl with a desire to be great
With the gifts God laid before her face
Gap toothed, a contagious smile
Inherited from her mother, passed down from her mother's
mother
Fears smothered
By her ability to pray to a God that lives in her thoughts
Heart and soul
A beauty
With a big forehead, where her crown sits
Royalty, dripped in the finest diamonds and jewels
That Black Beauty is me
Lines and marks where my skin stretched
Beautiful imperfections
An Ideal Model for an artist to sketch
Reaping the fruits of my planted seeds
Kind-hearted giver of myself to those in need
Black queen, success at my fingertips, the world under my toes
Through my words, my wisdom will be exposed
Shining on the outside, my slip won't be seen
Confident in all my imperfections
I'm in control of my self-esteem
Young mother, raising Queens to inherit the Kingdom
I've prepared before them
Perfectly selected as one of God's gems
In him I will do Great things

Part One:
Love Inspired

Brown Queens

From my womb, the birth of Queens
To live a dream not sold on America's Street Corners
Not birthed by Society, they'll show no love
Birthed into Royalty, their kingdom waiting in the clouds above
Young Queens, brown flesh, thick lips and curly locks
The world at the palms
Invested in education a stock that won't drop
My Queens privileged
Made in my image
Their faces stained with their mother's beauty
Brown Queens, destined for great things
Luxuries of life
College degrees
Marriage rings
All for these Brown Queens
Rich is wisdom
Crowned in Knowledge
Jeweled with Success
Well Polished
Take your place on your throne
My Brown Queens
Your time is now

Unclothed

Lying together
Cuddled together
Together we move
Together we touch
Together our eyes lock
Together we bond
Together we share a kiss
Lying together
Together our hands meet
Fingers interlocked
Together we laugh
Together we smile
Together in love
A nose kiss
Together we unite
Lying Unclothed
Together in Intimacy
Together we embrace
Together we sing
Connected together at the soul
Cuddled together
We fall asleep together
Unclothed

False Prophets

She wants to be loved is that so hard to ask for
While men rather see how their lips feel between her legs
They pretend to be interested in the words that flow out of her
soft brown lips,
See she never asked for much,
But honesty, but what does she get
A little bit of the opposite
Are they all to blame
Maybe, maybe not
See her body is a temple
She knows that all to well
The temple that many men have visited
Praises go up while they are deep inside her temple
But once they leave
They curse her temple
See when you are used to being worshipped
And your temple adored
You blame those who entered under false pretense
Are they solely responsible for destroying her temple
Maybe, maybe not
The doors have been closed until this temple goes through
renovation

Forbidden Fruit

Step into a world full of pleasure and fantasy
Taste the sweet juices of a forbidden fruit
One bite and you're hooked forever in a world that should
remain a secret
I wandered into this secret world by accident
Or shall I say by temptation
Temptation led me to this one special fruit whose sweet
ambiance drew me close
The closer I get the more I want to taste
To taste a fruit I was forbidden to touch
It tempted
I touched
It called
I surrendered
I gave in I was physically attracted to this one forbidden fruit
Forbidden to embrace
Forbidden to kiss
Forbidden to love
I reverenced on the taste and fed upon its ripeness
It wants me and I want more of it
So pure and endearing, admirable, loving and full of taste
Where would this fruit lead me?
I'm hooked forever and in this secret world I shall remain to
taste and feed upon my fruit
No one will ever know the truth

T.M.B

(Tears.Memories.Breaking-Free)

Tears fall down my soft cheeks as I figure out
Why Love has not
Found me yet
Hurt fills my heart and pierced my soul
The empty promises, no the false promises to care and
To make me happy all flew away when I
Opened up the window of my heart and soul
The games of life
I'm the one following the rules but yet I never win
Too much given, not much required, no ones fault but my own
I should have made you responsible for your words
And made sure your actions spoke for them
Everyone knows a broken-heart can be mended
But how do you mend a broken soul
Every time you lost yourself deep inside me
My soul tied itself to you
The love we made
The kisses to my lips
The passion
The flow of water from my body through my eyes each time
Each time my soul connected to yours
And I come into myself and my body shakes
I feel your love all over me
Memories, forever stained in my head
Thoughts of family and forever
My soul weeps for you,
I have to break free from you
I need to be released from you

Come Close

Her lips call out to you, her voice but a whisper
She needs you, tears fall
She is crying for you
You rise up as blood pumps through your muscles
You're ready to be there for her
She allows you in
Inside
She hugs you close
Tight
Squeezing every inch of you
You love the warmth of her spirit
You stay near
Inside you speak to her mental
Calm words
Slow
You move slow inside
Fragile
You take your time with her
Gentleness
She needs you
Bring her to a sacred place
Allow her to be free with you
She needs you
You need her too
You become one with her
Together you lead each other to paradise

Secrets Within Us

We're bonded together by him
He is the link between us
I secretly adore you, while you secretly lie with me
We secretly share one thing, intense passion, love-making and
intimacy
This affair is more than exciting, I can't deny it
My insides scream your name, they won't keep quiet
A deep sexual rush, my heart smiles with every touch
You're apart of me and I'm apart of you, stuck together like glue
Secrets we keep trapped down inside
We cover the truth with a blanket of lies
To protect him from heartache and broken trust
We remain silent, and mouths are shut
Thoughts of him get lost when we escape to our secret place
Make love to me baby, I love the way these secrets taste
No regrets
I'm forever grateful to him for linking me to you

Test and Trials

Test and trials to figure out where my heart lay
It lays at your mercy
What a huge wage to pay
The need to feel you close, I lost my sight in what's right
My heart leads me and I find myself in a sorry plight
Questions cloud my thoughts on what went wrong between us
I knew you were the one, my heart allowed me to trust
Yet yours doesn't, you're changing, summer is now winter
Your coldness is raging
Affection the bare minimal, love doesn't live here
Longing for gentle touches, to slow my tears
Rejection a relationships downfall, I needed you close
You left me alone and alone I should leave you I suppose
Test and Trials to see where your heart lays
No longer with me
Fighting to receive your love is now a wage
I'm just unwilling to pay

Our Meeting Place

Flower petals beneath my feet
Candles burning a smell so sweet
Soft flesh my body greets
Against the wall our privates meet
Deep breaths and moans
In me he has grown
Beyond submission
He leads me to a new position
Beneath my body his flesh lay
I grind slowly my hips sway
Warm hands massage cold cheeks
His stomach soaked as she secretes
Lips connect tongues embrace
Peeking at his handsome face
Our meeting intensifies
Hips gyrating up and down
Loud tones from the orgasms we both found
Naked flesh
Candles burning
No one moves or utters a sound

Indecisive

I've been toying with this decision
For quite some time now
Knowing what I needed to do but I couldn't
Disgusted by your attitude and nonchalant demeanor
I needed to make my decision
But something in me wouldn't allow me
To follow through just yet
Missing what we use to be
How you use to make me feel
I couldn't let go
I knew that my decision needed to be made
I didn't want to lose you
I felt a connection to you
That I couldn't part ways with
My heart and mind battling daily
My mind made up but my heart was indecisive
This was wrong
The right thing to do
Means walking away permanently

Emptiness in my Heart

Emptiness in my heart
I need to fill it with your love
Wanting to end up at the same destination
Yet the roads we travel aren't the same
I want you near
Without you my heart just doesn't feel the same
It hurts
Crushed as if a million elephants have trampled over it
My heart hurts
I'm breathing but there's no oxygen flowing to my heart
My life is in you
I breathe you
I need you
Feeling alone
My heart is in pieces
I want happiness
But I can't figure out which pieces to put together first
Never thought I'll be without you
How do I live each minute of each day
Of each month without you
How would I go on?
If I am no longer able to live from your love
Come back to me
Let the road you're traveling bring you back to me
If not for forever
Let it be for a second
Just to feel your love again

Equally Yoked

Pour yourself into me
Nourish my soul with your love
Give me you
I'll give you me
I'm falling
Be prepared to catch me
I'm swimming in your love
I'm not ready to reach the shore
Build with me
An empire of love
For us and our family
Devoted
Committed
Understanding
Kind
Patient
In love
A covenant under God
Equally yoked
Soul partners
Feed me with your love
Fill my belly with your love
Fill my spirit with your love
I'll pour myself into you
We intertwine at the soul
We nourish each other's strengths
Passion
Love
A bond
An unspeakable bond
An Equally Yoked Kind of Love

Tales of Hell on Earth

I have tales to tell about how he was out chasing tail
How he enslaved my mind in this emotional jail
Caged in a cell, not enough strength to place my own bail

I have tales to tell about the lumps on my head the size of hail
The strikes to my back the length of walking trails
I have tales to tell about how he would purposely let me fail
Disconnected me from the world so I couldn't excel
In hell, for the name of love, I lived in hell
Sold myself for cheap, he bought my soul at a clearance sale

I have tales to tell about a body so weak and frail
How he hand fed me food to control the numbers on the scale
How I laid on top of tables to vacuum out human cells
Every time my belly swelled

I have tales to tell about the weakness of this male
How he raped me daily and filled my body with his urine and
sperm
I was his human dumpster pail, trash

I have tales to tell how he was assailed by doubts
So he beat me unconscious he nailed me to the cross
How he dragged me through the fiery pits of hell
The left over blood on my lips
I've never tasted something so stale

I have tales to tell about a naked flesh, skin so flushed and pale
How he searched me daily
Like cattle he inspected me with detail

In hell, I lived in hell, we inhaled cocaine by the pail, an
addiction so strong

I have tales to tell about how he was out chasing tail
How he verbally accused me and abused me with each syllable
he yelled
I was living in hell on Earth

I have tales to tell about a woman, who finally prevailed,
How she saved up enough strength to place her own bail
How she defeated the devil and ran out of hell
And broke free from her mental cell
A woman now at ease, a woman who could finally exhale

Hooked on Love

Addicted to your touch
Addicted to your smell
Addicted to how you lift me closer to God
Addicted to your strength
Addicted to your smile
Addicted to your voice a soothing tone
Addicted to the way you love
Addicted to your dream and goals
Addicted to your soft lips
Addicted to your kiss
Addicted to your ability to provide
I'm in love

I'm addicted to your love
I'm hooked forever
I'm addicted to your love
Loving you is my heaven

Addicted to your unselfishness
Addicted to the way your body moves during our intimate dance
Addicted to your ability to lead without fear
Addicted to how you place me first above all others
Addicted to you
I'm in love

I'm Addicted to your love
I'm hooked forever
I'm addicted to your love
Loving you is like heaven

The Great Spot

Laying down my mind starts to wonder to a place
I'm too familiar with, my happy place
My place of bliss and joy
Fingers on my thighs
Fingers on my thighs tiptoeing to my inner place
Gasp! I'm here
I'm back, let me catch my breath
The aroma, the warmth
The peace, back to witness the flowing of water
The streams of angelic water so pure and sweet
Tiptoeing through the tightest caves and making their way
through sticky ponds
In search of The Great Spot
Tiptoeing turns into hard footsteps
They race to The Great Spot
Faster, they run faster to this magical spot
The Great Spot, they found it
They start dancing, hard thrusting movements, they begin to
march one finger after another they find a deep rhythm
The Great spot is impressed
More dancing, Rhythmic motions
Dance for The Great Spot
Reverence and love The Great Spot
The Great Spot is pleased
Something unspoken, unexplained
Orgasmic has taken place
My legs are shaking, my thighs soaked, my sheets drenched
Finger sticky
I'm at ease, ecstasy
Pure love
And It's all me

18

Far Too Long

Too long I stayed too long
I should have left way before we decided to birth a child
The emotional affairs, the humiliation, I stayed to long
We fought a never-ending battle where no one was winning
I needed the fairytale of love, the high school sweetheart tale
To share with my kids and their kids
That fairytale kept me there far too long.
Every time you seeked comfort in others
Ice covered my heart, I grew cold
I had to prove something to these women that I won you
By sending childish messages that I was the one you loved
Laughter, they laughed at how pitiful and insecure I was
Leaving,would've meant they would've won
I couldn't have that so I stayed
And you made me your wife, out of obligation to our child
In love with the idea and in love with you
I believed we did the right thing
A marriage rocky from the start, starting a new
Yet the past seems to follow us
Wanting to throw in the towel but the thoughts of being another
Black Single mother
Was a statistic I didn't want attached to my name
Afraid that God wouldn't forgive me if I left
I stayed and I was miserable
For better or for worse
But this was far beyond the worse I was willing to take
Several straws broke the camel's back and being happy seemed
More important than the thoughts of others.
I couldn't stay much longer, I deserved to be happy
I needed to free myself
So I did

Who Are We

I'm unsure of what you have bestowed upon me
Feelings floating in a sea of uncertainty
Uncertainty at a time
Just a time where my words may not find you
Distance between us
Us
Who are we together?
Who are we apart?
Walls built from bricks of pain, sadness and disloyalty
A shield to protect a heart that can't take another beating
From you
My heart beats for you
A rhythm that flows like a calm river off the coast of east Africa
Pure
My love was pure
No filtration
No toxins
Purified love
Love that pumped energy into your body
Body and mind
You polluted your mind
Filling it with toxic thoughts of lustful women
Women your body entered into, into these women you came
And you came back into my body filling it with polluted toxins
I'm uncertain if this is love,
Who are we together?
A broken record
The music a beautiful melody
But there are still broken cracks in our love that will never heal
Who are we apart?
Just two individuals craving for real love

Drifting Away

Drifting away, I packed my bags as I prepared to leave.
You grab my bags and unpacked them claiming without me you
couldn't breathe
Almost gone, one foot out the door
You begged me to try once more
You unpacked my trust and put it in the drawer
Unpacked my heart
With that came a promise of a new start
Happiness in my spirit over the last couple of days
But that wouldn't last
You were back to your old ways
A disconnect I felt with every touch, reminds me
Why I shouldn't love you so much
Drifting away with thoughts of misery
Anything for you, you were always my top priority
Selfish in your actions, you knew you wouldn't change
Fake proposals to ease my mind
You would never give me your last name
Drifting away to a place of contentment
My heart is no longer your residence you have been evicted
I had love for you but a deeper love for myself
No longer a trophy to have displayed on your shelf
Drifting away to a new beginning
Fell in love with myself
Oh how wonderful it feels to be winning

Dinner for Two

I finished my last bite of food as we dined at our favorite spot
the music was great, the wine has me feeling hot
Every table full, a busy Saturday night
I look your way, impressed by what I see
I wanted your fullness deep inside me
I make my way to the bathroom, you follow behind
A connection so strong, I'm almost sure you've read my mind
I peek inside the bathroom, the coast was clear
Into the stall you pull me near
We share a kiss full of tongue and passion
Neglected our table for some bathroom romancing
Soft kisses to my neck down to my spine
He lifts up my Skirt and enters from behind
His thickness delighted by my warm invitation
I tighten my muscles to feel each stroke of penetration
Noises fill the air people file into the bathroom
I couldn't let him stop, it would've been too soon
Filled with adrenaline, he doesn't stop
I moan a little louder
I secretly want them to hear me
As we make love in this restaurant, one of my deepest fantasies
The intensity builds, I'm ready for release
The bathroom is crowded
The deeper he goes my moans increase
I reach my cloud nine, we meet at the finish line
The sound of silence fills the air
What an ideal love affair
I sneak out the bathroom he follows behind
Every ounce of me pleased that he read my mind
Back to our seats everything just right
A dinner for two in this restaurant on a busy Saturday night

My First Rap Song
(Teenage Love 2003)

He was eighteen, my young love, and a cutie
And to give him what he wants was my duty
He was it, my number one pick
Never thought he messed around with so many chicks
I kept it real, something he could never do
But if he wanted the world
I think I want it to
What was I supposed to do?
He was fine
One of a kind
Truth is love was blind
How could this be?
I gave him everything that he needed
He wasn't cocky, maybe just a little conceited
I should've seen it, it was an act
I thought I needed him but I don't want him back

I Love You

I love you
You are consistent in my life
My strength
My provider
I love you
Not because I was taught to believe in you
It's because I believe in you
In my heart I keep you
Forgiving
Chastise me when I'm wrong
Speak to my heart, lead me to do right
You love me more than I can ever imagine
I love you Jesus
Thank you for loving me
Even when I do wrong
You still care
Even when I am stubborn
You're still there
Even when I feel like giving up
You give me that extra push to go on
I love you Lord
Thank you for loving me
First

Cursed

Indescribable plagues
Cursed from the beginning
Inside crystal balls
A prophesy that evil things are yet to come
Warning comes in the morning
Destruction meets us in the evening
Buried in tombs a love that needed to be put to rest
Seeking answers for this relationships demise
We resurrect a love that was meant to die
Bruises left behind from the pieces of broken glass
Inside this broken mirror are two broken reflections
Trying to piece together a puzzle with no pieces
This thing isn't fixable
Broken lights
Darkness seem to find us
We are cursed
Warning comes in the morning
So I'll be sure to bury us in the evening

Definition of Insanity
(Part one)

The madness, the anger, the phone calls, the emails, the
pregnancies, the other woman
We have been doing this dance for a while now, The same tired
old two step, trying to keep you home, but you rather roam on
the other side of town

Through your phone I search for numbers and texts,
Prove that you're cheating and you're out having sex
662-9319, I dialed her number like I've done some many times
She answers politely and she says "Hello"
I asked where was Angelo
She snickers a bit and says yes, he's here
I release the call and I shed a few tears

This is madness, this was anger I felt, I buckle up my seatbelt
Looking at the cards I've been dealt
Six years, three kids and one other woman, after all this fighting
I'm supposed to be winning
My bed is for you and I
For us to make love and for our souls to tie

I'm racing to her house, the 7th time this week,
To get my man, in our bed is where you should be asleep
I reach for my nine like I've done so many times
I have a lot more courage, my mind is getting sicker
To end her life, all I have to do is pull the trigger

My competition in the flesh
I hated her, why was he so obsessed
Her eyes red, she begged me not to
My mind made up, I had to follow through
I owe you nothing you deserve the repercussions for his sin
I think finally this time, I may win

I send one bullet in her head, she falls to the ground
His face full of shock, he doesn't utter a sound

On my way over I also decided to assign a bullet to his name
His lack of love drove me insane
"She met nothing to me baby,
I promise, it just you and I", he said
"You see I didn't even cry
When you sent that bullet through her head"

Your colder than I thought, a little sicker than me
I can't stop, your bullet is now ready for delivery
I gave him one last kiss to the side of his face
And asked him to repent and pray for God's grace

Six bullets to your legs for the years
You would never stand up for me
Three to your penis
For those three bastard children you had with me
One to your heart
Where you should've kept me and only me

I fled the scene and left him by the side of his wife
It's a shame how after all these years, you never gave me her life
I told everyone, I was his wife, the one who took vows
That I was linked to him under God's covenant
And she was the home wrecker, but that was the title I represent
I am her and she is me, the same old dance
Hoping to get a different man

Cold blooded, I was now a killer
Wanted a fairytale love, but all I got was a thriller
Insane this was, insane I became

Just for a piece of a man, who wouldn't give me his last name
Alone in my bed and I have nothing to show for it
Just a life of deceit, pain and despair
I also assigned a bullet to my own name
Shot myself in the heart
Just for a piece of a man
I became the definition of Insane

Definition of Insanity
(Part 2)

I met Angelo, one night at the bar
I was dancing with my girls, we locked eyes from afar
Tall, brown skin cutie, his look was mesmerizing
The things I could do to him, oh my, he had me fantasizing
He approached me for a dance; I seduced him with my moves
And in sync, we grooved

He stayed joined by my side the entire night
He requested that I join him for dinner tomorrow, by candlelight
His thick lips and his smile bright
I happily obliged him on his invite
We exchanged numbers with plans for tomorrow
I was ready to get back out there, to erase my sorrow

Everything was going according to plan
And if this date goes well, I anticipate on making him my man
Until I noticed the ring on his left hand
The date ended, everything went well
A little upset about what he chose not to tell
He kissed me goodnight
I didn't kiss back
I had to inquire about his wife

He said he has been married for three years things weren't good
The sex was lacking and she often challenged his manhood
He said she was ungrateful
She didn't work and he paid all the bills
What she wouldn't do, I'll be the woman who will
I took that as my personal challenge to make up for the things
she lacked

I'm the cleanup woman, he'll never go back
So foolish of her to neglect a good man

If I play my cards right, I'll have that finger on my hand
So I thought……

Definition of Insanity
(Part 3)

Hair pulling, neck biting, intensity and passion
His hands on my body, he loved caressing
I climb on top, he slid into wetness
With me there was no stress
We was suddenly interrupted by the sound of his phone
I immediately knew who it was by the special ringtone
She needed him home
It's been three years, so I'm use to the routine
Promises to leave her but yet she still wears the ring
He wouldn't even finish what we started
He gave me three kisses and told me he loved me as we parted

Angelo was in love with me, things were complicated
I knew exactly where he wanted to be
He had so much to lose if he left right away
So he had to leave strategically so he wouldn't have to pay
Alimony
He didn't love her, I had his heart
They had two children, which made it tougher to split apart

Angelo also birthed a child with me
A son, Angelo jr. named after his daddy
Vacations and family trips, I was living well
Shopping sprees,
And money by the pail
I did my job and hers too
When they bought a new home, I got one too
Patient with him, the timing was just off
When this was all over she would be the one at a lost
He loved me
So I thought.....

Definition of Insanity
(Part 4)

I was twisted to think that this was love, I still shared his time
Three more years, and two more kids with a man that wasn't
mine
My patience wearing thin, I needed my man
Being his mistress for six years wasn't part of the plan
I gave him all the fantasies his wife rejected
How to please this man, I had that perfected
I was his encouragement, when he was down
I pulled him back up
Yet I'm the one getting all the bad luck

He stopped making payments on the house that we bought
And things were getting worse, every day we fought
I lost the house and he moved me and the children into his
father's basement
I didn't questioned his decision or how his money was spent
because I never had to be responsible for paying the rent

Three months go by and we grew a little closer, things calmed all
the way down
He started spending more than two nights on my side of town
Just when I thought his promises could be empty
I read a beautiful text he sent me
It read "Baby its time, I'm ready to leave her behind
you're half of my soul, and it's you I choose"
Elated my heart began to sing
I was finally getting my man and my ring
Until
He delivered some bad news

That right now wouldn't be a good time to leave, because somehow
His wife had conceived, another child
What has he done to me, what happen to our family?
He will soon be mine even if it's involuntarily

Definition of Insanity
(Part 5)

All these years I've wasted for this man
Waiting around hoping to have a diamond on my hand
In my mind I had become the wife and she was his mistress
And I needed a way to get rid of this chick
He choose not to follow through with the promises he made
Tired of being a pawn in his wicked game

Insane he drove me
Insane I drove myself
I thought if I love him better, he would leave
If thought if I sexed him better, he would leave
I thought if I was always a step ahead of her, he would leave
I thought my support and encouragement made me better and he
would leave
I signed up for this I know I did
But that's beside the point now
Why did he make her his wife?
I don't even know why he took those vows
Just to have a mistress for six years of his life

What was I lacking that kept him in that marriage?
That kept him bonded to her and not to me?
What type of love was she offering?
That kept him from leaving her and marrying me?

I hate her, I do, I hate her with my soul
She wasn't half the woman I was
I made him happy
I gave him children
I gave him six years of my life
I needed him

I was going insane, she needed to disappear
I think I may have lost my mind
Bought me a gun, the other day
I think it's time, I take a ride
I'm going to get what's mine

The Arrival of an Angel

I've heard stories about the parties in heaven
You could only attend by invitation
God has personally invited you this time to take part in this
celebration
He planned it perfectly
Detailed in every way
A celebration in heaven
For you on your 67th birthday
He brought you there peacefully
During your mid-day slumber
Stripped away the sickness and depression
For eternal happiness and comfort

What an entrance you make
You're the star of the show
A flawless beauty
Make-up on your face painted by God
A long white Gown
Accessorized with wings
And a halo for your head that glows
The angels rejoice
Upon your arrival
A renewing of your soul
A heavenly revival

The trumpets sound
The angels are dancing
For this is a joyous time
A celebration of life
For a woman so sweet and divine
Laugh now grandma
Reverence in your peace of mind

Beautiful woman
Genuine and blessed

Your spirit fills our hearts
Even when we will no longer be able to feel your flesh
Your home now
You're living amongst the best
I shed a few tears
I smile
I find an inner peace
Knowing your soul is finally at rest

Rest in Heaven Grandma

In Loving Memory Of

Barbara Jo Trimble
Feb. 2, 1947 – Feb. 2, 2014

Part Two
Life Inspired

Inspired by LIFE

The lights are bright, the crowd is thick
They bought tickets to my show
They patiently wait for my words
My thoughts
My wisdom about life
The curtains are drawn back
The music is cued
My pen is ready to dance across my paper

This show is about life, and inspiration
My pen does this dance quite often because life is full of
happiness, sadness and sexuality
The birth of a baby, the death of a love one
Each moment leads my pen to dance
Love, real love, oh how beautiful it is to write about love,
Hearts filled with love
Hearts broken
My pen dances for the broken hearts too
My pen dances for the struggling
The unspeakable,
Inspired by God, inspired by people
My pen is inspired by life

I write about things that affect me personally
I write about things that may not relate to me
I'm inspired by how these things affect other people
I need my pen to move for me
Like waves move in the ocean
A flow, my pen flows with my thoughts
My life, your life inspires my writing
My pen doesn't dance only for me but for those
Who may need just a little bit of Life's Inspiration

Sunrise

There is something special about a sunrise
The light of a new day,
The strength to take new strides
There is something special about a sunrise
A new start, darkness only for a while
Joy surely comes in the morning
The sun rises up, the birds are singing
The fish are swimming
There is something special about a sunrise
Another chance at life
A present full of hope and faith
A renewing of peace in our spirit
There is something special about a sunrise
When the sun rise up and a new day has begun
It is our time to start living better
Forget about yesterday and what was or what it could have been
and focus on the beauty of a new day
There is something so special about a sunrise

Keeping up with the Jones'

Living way above their means
They go into debt chasing the Jones' dreams
They brag about spending five hundred dollars on a pair of jeans
So they can look like the Jones' when they hit the scene
They don't want to seem cheap
So they buy Michael Kors, to wear on their shoulders and feet
Pay check to pay check light bill past due
Bill money is spent at the club to pop bottles like the Jones' do
They won't shop at Wal-Mart because they aren't expensive
enough
True Religion gets their money even though they can't afford
that stuff
Eviction notices and cars repossessed
Don't know the importance of savings
These things aren't being stressed
So they spend all their money to afford their way of dress
To impress, those who could careless
Bouncing checks and back in poverty
This isn't the type of lifestyle for the wealthy
A fairy tale in their head that all the wealthy and rich spend
money frivolously
You can't get rich if you don't save any money
They see the Jones' and they try to keep up with their life
Yet they fail to see all the sacrifices they made so they can live
nice
It's about time to stop looking rich and put in the work to be rich
Spending like Money Roebucks
But living in a good times apartment
Living a life full of debt
If your goal is to live well and afford many homes
Please stop going broke, trying to keep up with the Jones'

Betrayals of Masculinity

Hurt by the one who should've remained
A young boy trapped in his own pain
Raised by his father, rejected by his mother
He played around with the hearts of others
Brought up tough, men never show emotion
So in his relationships he lacked devotion
Encouraged to play the field
One main course and a dish on the side
Commitment foreign, he could never abide
By his relationships

Men were strong, that's what he learned about this world
Until he was knocked off his feet by this one particular girl
His love for her grew from the moment they met
But the commitment he promised her, he would soon forget
This love thing was for women
These weren't the feelings of men
Temptation called
He answered and always gave in

The love he had for her was deeper than before
He loved her smile and her personality he just simply adored
She was who he needed at the time
But he neglected those feelings, he paid them no mind
And allowed other women to occupy his time

She grew tired of the infidelity she walked out of his life
Another one will come
He thought so he let go without thinking twice
He searched for other women to take her place
No other woman was able to put that type of smile on his face
The loss of a first love, brought his heart no contentment
He lost a love because being emotionless was more important

His own vanity
Caused him to be betrayed by his own masculinity

Violated

Her skirt tight and short
Her cleavage peeping out of a shirt that is thin
He used that as an excuse to force his way in
He said she seduced him by the way she was dressed
He felt she gave him an open invitation to come and have sex
A predator starving to feast on his prey
He followed her every move
She was now ready to lay
He held her mouth shut, he ripped apart her skirt
He pushed his way inside no matter the amount of hurt
She begged and pleaded
Ignoring her screams, he finished his deed
He left her broken abused and alone
Nobody to cry out for she was too far from home

Her hair tied
Relaxed she was out washing clothes
In her baggy shirt and sweatpants
He came closer to sweet talk her, hoping she'll give him a chance
He made his move she politely declined
Upset because she said no for the third time
Feeling uneasy about her rejection, he pushed over top of the
machine and VIOLATED her without any protection
Her loud screams go unanswered
No one around to free her from this human cancer
She begged and pleads, he ignored her and finished his deed
He left her broken, abused and alone
Nobody to cry out to she was too far from home

Rape is never about the victim and how she was dressed
It's about the rapist and the demons they possess
A woman should feel safe in shorts or in pants
Her lack clothing shouldn't be a rapist invite to dance

44

The victims should no longer be the one society blames and
make these abusers accountable for their victim's long-life of
pain
This is for the women who may have been here before
No matter the circumstance, you are not at fault for someone
uninvited to come through your door
I pray for your strength and in time healing for the best
You don't deserved to be VIOLATED
No matter how you are dressed

Young and Wild

Young and wild
Living life careless and fast
Promises to these young girls, that he'll be their last
He met a young girl, thick in all the right places
Thoughts of only sex, he wanted to see her private places
He smoothed talked his way into her heart
Visions of entering, where her thighs part
She let him indulge in her honey spot
A taste so sweet, he savored every last drop
Kissing and grinding the power of lust
Unprotected, in him she trust

Young and wild
Caught up in the moment
He asked her to mother his child
He released himself, the process begins
Her egg fertilized, by one drop of his semen
Her belly big and plump and full of life
They argued daily, conversations full of strife
No money, No job he was up to no good
Still out chasing women, unprepared for fatherhood

Young and Wild
With each passing month, he became distant
She begged for support, each plea he resisted
Nine months gone, forced into twenty-two hours of labor alone
She birthed a son, who inherited his father's genes
A son that was never part of his father's dreams
He finally showed up, to give his last name,
A son, his mother's joy, his father's pain

Young and Wild
Living life without a care in the world

Forgetting the promises he made to that young girl
Deadbeat, daddy is beat down
Careless, he sowed three more seeds across town
Carriages, several baby carriages
Different mothers, same father
Not one child birthed in the bonds of marriage

Young and wild
A vicious cycle he repeated over and over again
These fatherless children paying for their father's sin
Karma, catching up with him, he didn't dream of this type of life
Still living with the repercussions of making her a mother before
he made her his wife

Memories of a Father's Decisions

She just a girl, so sweet and kind
A young girl not even ten years old
She longs to please her daddy
Anything to make him happy for she feared his anger
He loved his daughter but he was afraid she would get the best
of him
She needed him to listen to her without rejection
She needed his love, not because he provided for her
But because she was a piece of his soul
She cries sometimes because she is scared to disappoint him
She doesn't understand some of her father decisions
Because her father still battles with the decisions of his father

He's just a boy so sweet and kind
a young boy not even ten years old
He longs to please his daddy
Anything to make him happy for he feared his anger
His father loved his son but he was afraid he would get the best
of him
He needed him to listen to him without rejection
He needed his love, not because he provided for him
But because he was a piece of his soul
He cries sometimes because he is scared to disappoint him
He doesn't understand some of the decisions of his father and
those decisions of his father have now trickled down to that
sweet little girl

Her father must break the cycle with love and forgiveness
And an understanding that the past can't be changed
Her father must decide that the decisions of his father
Will not be present in his love for his daughter
She's crying out to him
She needs more of her father
A relationship and not just his presence

For when she grows up and reflect back on her father, she will be elated that he made good decisions in how he
Chose to love her

Big Girls Don't Cry

They say big girls don't cry
I have to ask why
How do I cleanse my soul?
When my heart is in pieces and I need to feel whole
Crying washes away the pain
Helps me to find peace with the things I couldn't change

The say big girls don't cry
I have to ask why
I'm not weak because I cry, with every tear I grow strong
Crying is my sweet harmony to this emotional song

They say big girls don't cry
I have to ask why
Crying is the joy you feel when a baby is born
Or when he makes you his Queen and with jewels your hand is
adorned
Crying when I'm happy and in sweet bliss
Knowing in the midst of a storm,
My God got this

They say big girls don't cry
I have to ask why
Should my tears be held captive by my eyes?
A big girl I am
I have to ask why
Should I be afraid to cry?

Digging for Gold

Mansions and pools, vacations in the tropics
Dreams in her head and every conversations topic
A life she knew she couldn't provide for herself
She bargained with her vagina to secure her wealth
Starving for a taste of the good life
For what she had planned, she would be guaranteed his money
without having to be his wife

She was going to make him a father without his consent
So she could shop in Paris, while he paid her rent
He was a good man, headed in the right direction
Seeing his fortune, she poked holes in the protection
Full of scandal and deception,
She was chasing the money train, hoping for conception
In love with his money, she became obsessed
4 negatives, she couldn't get one positive pregnancy test

Determined to gain his fortune, a new plan in place
To get pregnant is the goal,
Hoping her scandalous activities wouldn't be traced
Finally she's pregnant; she's overwhelmed with joy and
excitement
Thoughts of money in her bank from the child support payment
Three months in but this pregnancy wouldn't last
A weak uterus, results from her abortions in the past
Devastated at what was now before her
She needed that child to help her finances get better

For a life of luxury, she was more than willing to scheme
Just to have a piece of the American Dream
Too lazy to acquire the money by her own work ethics
She would lay with men and they supplied the basics
But that child was her golden ticket, the money was guaranteed

He never wanted kids, she knew that when they met
She didn't care about his feelings
She needed his money to afford her diamond baguettes
Her manipulations wouldn't succeed
That golden ticket was no longer guaranteed
He didn't want her to carry his seed
After he found text messages revealing her greed
He left her broke without a penny to her name
She needed to get money, she was back in the game

Back on the market, she auctioned her vagina to the highest bid
In hopes of birthing at least one rich man's kid
Let the scheming begin,
Seducing these men so they would spend

A lost girl
Even with her materials she'll never feel whole
For the Love of money she sold her soul
Jumping from men to men, she spent her whole life
Digging for gold

Faith

On my knees, praying looking for a way out of this dark place
where is the love?
Trials causing me to lose faith in the man above
I Cry out "oh lord why me"
He speaks out "Why not you,
In you, others will see my glory"
Finally made it to the top of the mountain
Yet I seem to fall back down
Thirsty, yet I find myself sipping from the devil's fountain
Still waiting for you to make blessing rain down for me
My faith in question
As I watch other suffers, who gave you their loyalty
My father, why should I suffer at your hands?
I should be further
According to my plans
I turned my life around, I'm finally doing right
But I find myself alone and I'm still losing sight
Searching for answers, everything is so cliché
Speak to me Lord, let your light lead the way
Show your face Lord, I need you
To restore my faith
In all that you do
Lead me towards your truth and understanding
To feed upon you
Cover me with your hand
Come into my heart and make yourself at home
I need to get to know you for myself
I need you to restore my faith

American Girl

African American
I am American
My history captured in textbooks
History,
His story,
Her story
Whose story am I to believe?
Assigned the title of African
Yet I've never planted my feet on African soil
Some Africans won't embrace me
Because in their eyes, I'm not African,
I'm American
Born American
But his story says these aren't my native roots
Families torn apart
The wickedness of slavery
Who are my Ancestors?
Kings and Queens sitting on thrones in high places
Or American Natives some call Indians
Birth certificates manipulated
Names changed
His story changed,
Labels to separate me from my own birthplace
Am I a descendant of a slave?
Have my people always been free?
American hyphenate African
I'm not denying who I am
His story just doesn't fully tell me who I am
Inventors are my people inventors
Stop lights and peanut butter
My people were destined for great things
Call me American
Are my people African?
Are my people European?

Are my people Native Americans?

In essence I'm mixed with all those things
But American is who I am
My culture
My way of life
I am black
But my color doesn't define who I am
Or dictate who I will become
My color only tells you my descendants could be African,
American and no, I don't have to hyphenate the African
Accept that I am just as American as my counterparts
His story tells you a little about me
But that isn't my whole story
Please don't cheat me
I am black and I am American
And my story is still being written

In the Midst of Chaos

Emotions run high
Feelings still fresh
Children in the midst of chaos
A romantic relationship ended
Some just won't let go to form a new relationship
Co-Parenting
Children suffering for the selfish acts of their parents
The mother becomes the focus
Her whereabouts
Who she's seeing
The children become an after thought
Fatherhood becomes a babysitting service
Dads are now watching their kids
Clocking the amount of hours being spent
As if those children aren't even theirs
No court orders of child support
Or visitation
The father is given the benefit of the doubt
Yet that's too much for him
Angry at the mother he takes it out on the children
No phone calls to check on his children's well-being
No time being spent to bond
Losing focus on what's important
His immaturity getting the best of him
He love his children
But not with his whole heart
Because if he did nothing would get in the way
Of him being present in his children's life
No matter if him and the mother lived apart
Mother's upset because the father moved on
So now she uses the children as pawns
Against their father
He can't see his kids

If he doesn't want to be with her
She won't allow him to live in peace
So she keeps up drama between him
And his new woman
Selfish, her wants become more important
Than the kid's needs
Blinded by her emotions
She doesn't see how her actions hinder
The relationship her children could have with their father

Y'all chose to sleep with each other and birth children
Why can't y'all make the choice to co-parent peacefully?
No matter the differences

Put yourself aside
It's no longer about you
It's about those children

And keeping their life as happy as it can be
Even if you live separately

Shaneka

Black Power
Fist tight raised in the air
We stand strong
Take out that relaxer
Unstitch those tracks
Let go of that weave
Be proud of that coarse thick afro
Shaneka
Shaneka?
Her mother named her that
Ugh that's ghetto and improper, they say
Your mother should have named you Ashley
We are our own enemy
Hypocrites in our own ways
We want our sisters to ignore America's beauty standards
But in the same breath we should follow America's standards
when it comes to names
We want our black sister's natural
Coarse roots
Wearing their natural curls
But we rather her be named Ashley than Shaneka
Because Shaneka isn't proper it sounds too ghetto
Confusing messages
They say be black and proud
Yet they say name your child something where on his resume a
future employer couldn't determine his race
Am I not supposed to be proud of who I am?
So why am I still afraid of future employers knowing
If I'm black or not
Promoting Prejudice
A lost people
In the back of some of our minds
We still aren't equivalent to our counterparts

Afraid that if they knew our race
We won't get the job

Be proud
Be black and proud
Ashamed of my own race
When I submit my resume
Because Ashley could be white
But Shaneka is most definitely black
And I most definitely don't want them to think
I'm black
Even if I graduated from a Top University and I'm highly
qualified that doesn't matter if they think I'm black
We will protest for the right to wear afros and dreads but will
close our mouths when they discriminate on someone because of
their name
Because it doesn't sound professional
They say afros look untamed and aren't professional
Yet we will go to bat to defend our beauty

If Shaneka said she had to straighten her hair to get the job
Most of you will turn your nose up and tell her not
To change herself for a job
But if she said she changed her name to Ashley in order for her
To get a job
Most will applaud her
Hypocrites
This is about the hypocrites who support discrimination
Prejudice is still real
But we have to stop giving them the power over us

Just because Shaneka isn't a typical American name
Doesn't mean it isn't a nice name or that she
Comes from the ghetto

Change starts when we stop taking jobs or assisting them in
throwing out resumes
Where we know they promote prejudice
Even if its prejudice against someone
Because of their name

This isn't to excuse the 15 letter names with random punctuation
and children named after foolishness
In that area some must do better

This is about hypocrites

Shanetta, Rayshaun, Ronique, Jermeka,Davion, Shaquanna
These name aren't typical American names but they aren't
ridiculous and over the top either
Even if it sounds "black" or "ethnic" they are still human
So they deserve a chance

So Shaneka, be proud of your name and your race
With God in your corner, you are still destined to be great.

About The Author

Born in Gary, Indiana and raised in Raleigh North Carolina. Bre'Yanna has always had a passion for writing poetry and short stories. A mother of two beautiful daughters Skye and Taighlor, they inspired her to pursue her passion of writing. Imperfect Greatness is her first published book.

Author's Contact

Bmparker05@gmail.com